Books by

HOWARD MOSS

A WINTER COME, A SUMMER GONE

A SWIMMER IN THE AIR

THE TOY FAIR

THE WOUND AND THE WEATHER

Edited by, with Introduction

KEATS

A WINTER COME, A SUMMER GONE.

POEMS 1946-1960

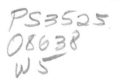

A WINTER COME,

A SUMMER GONE

POEMS 1946-1960

by

HOWARD MOSS

CHARLES SCRIBNER'S SONS   *New York*

The following poems were first published in *The New Yorker:* Bermuda, A Box at the Opera, Cry from Montauk, Dreams, The Dumb Show, Elizabethan Tragedy: A Footnote, Explorers, The Feast, Florida, The Gift to be Simple, The Hermit, If You Can, Light and Dark, Local Places, Mountain and Clouds, Rain, Salt-Water Taffy, Small Elegy, A Summer Gone, Torches, Tourists, The Truth About Love, Underwood, The Wind is Round, Winter's End, A Winter Come.

Other poems first appeared in *Botteghe Oscure* (ROME), *Briarcliff Quarterly, Chimera, Contemporary Poetry, Harper's, Harper's Bazaar, Hudson Review, Kenyon Review, Modern Writing, The Nation, New World Writing, Paris Review, Partisan Review, Perspectives, Poetry: A Magazine* of Verse, *Poetry London-New York, Poetry New York, Poetry Quarterly* (LONDON), *Saturday Review,* and *The Times Literary Supplement* (LONDON).

For SHIRLEY EVANS, MILDRED WOOD,

and ELIZABETH HANNUM

Contents

I

A WINTER COME

I

When frost moves fast and gardens lose their ground
And gold goes downward in the trees, no sound
Accompanies departures of the leaves,
Except when the wind hurtles into air
Dead shapes the coming winter will inter;
Then the thinnest music starts to stir
A faint, crisp scraping in the startled ear:
The leaves that feed the new leaves of next year.

II

Branch of a being that is bent by snow,
How many birds desert your stiffened bough?
There was a cage of lyrics in the air,
A bird for every leaf suspended there,
Who chirped at sunlight in the foliage
That farmed its summer at the meadow's edge;
And now an arm as thin as any wing
Rasps the iron air, bereft of song.

[3]

III

A child lay down in his imagined grave
To see the form he'd make engraved in snow,
But even that feigned hollow filled with snow;
And, rising on a landscape blurred a bit
By shadows of an adumbrated blue,
He came upon two worlds he had not known:
One was his being, one his mind let go
Until the light would take the blue from snow.

IV

Your breath precedes you on a winter's day,
An insubstantial cloud, as if to say,
All solid things are blown to vapor soon.
Look up! The scimitar of the moon
Is but a remnant of the round it was,
Is but a ringlet of the ring to be,
As, riding forth, the breath that marked your birth
Will have its heir, before it comes to death.

V

As birds come nearer for a crust of bread
Across the frozen snow, by hunger led
To stamp fine footprints on a scroll of white,
So winter is a world where appetite
Grows bolder by necessity, where the fox
Betrays his fable, and the cold unlocks
Stiff beggars from the doorways. Time grows old
In the knuckles of an old man blue with cold.

VI

The racing waterfall that slowed in fall
Has thinned to a trickle or an icicle
And stands as quiet as the rocks it willed
To move. As though expecting it to fall,
A listener stands upon a rim of silence,
Seeing a changed world prepared to change,
The waterfall silent on its breakneck shelf,
And silence a spectacle in itself.

VII

Adrift upon thin ice before he falls
Asleep is the sleeper deep in snow
That falls in imaginary winters in
The mind remembering the snow when no
Snow is falling, who will raise a blind,
Certain he has sensed its slow descent,
And find the crippled world he left behind,
And his transfiguration, in the mind.

VIII

Those statues, born long after funerals
Have mourned their subjects, stand in every park—
Stone statesmen stiff upon their pedestals,
Who dominate indifferent day and dark.
Blind to all the cruder jokes of snow,
A socket of sheer cold behind each eye,
They cannot know that even sculptors go
Where all the celebrated sitters lie.

IX

Who reads by starlight knows what fire is,
The end of words, and how its mysteries
Go running in the flame too quick to see,
As language has a light too bright to be
Mere fact or fiction. By ambiguity
We make of flame a word that flame can burn,
And of love a stillness, though the world can turn
On its moment, and be still. Or turn and turn.

X

And what of love that old men dead and gone
Have wintered through, and written messages
In snow so travelers, who come too warm
To what may grow too cold, be safe from harm?
They know the fire of flesh is winter's cheat
And how the icy wind makes young blood sweet
In joining joy, which age can never have.
And that is what all old men know of love.

II

DREAMS

If dreams were not the truth
But only things that come
From care or delirium—
A voice in a phone booth
Grown louder so the world
Might listen in to wrath—
Of love, I'd say, in truth,
We dream a dreaming world.

But nightly at our trades
Of reeling in the real,
The figures seem too real
Merely to be charades;
And love will not keep still,
Though wrath may hold its tongue;
In dreams we walk among
Our failures and fulfill

What every world of love
Demands: a dream made real.
And those who claim they feel

DREAMS

Nothing may come to love
Nothing and something more:
Dead leaves grown green again
On every tree they've slain
To live in metaphor.

We damn the scheming world.
The true world's in our dreams.
Reiterated themes
Unwind from where they're coiled
Inside the branching brain,
And each brain has a love
It might be dreaming of
That sleep may entertain.

And nightly, too, that love
Is dreaming somewhere else,
And cannot stop the pulse
Of both its wrath and love
From drawing images,
From all the worlds it has,
    Of how the world is,
    And how the world was.

THOSE WHO CANNOT ARE CONDEMNED

"Those who cannot remember the past
are condemned to repeat it."

SANTAYANA

Shipwrecked in daylight and docked in dark,
The blindman lacks a mirror in each eye,
But from the ticking clock and the crowing cock
He maps, in the dark, a visionary sky.
Seeing all the planets and the stars plain
Inside his head, and sensing the terrain,
He needs no walking stick to walk again.

No repetitions dawn, no slow-dimmed dusk
Distinguishes the darkness from the sun,
And though his world is uniformly black,
He sees realities in unison.
And there are those who see far less than he
By seeing more, and choose a twisted key
To lock themselves from their necessity.

For memory distorts the ghosts that ply
The glassy lightness of their mirrors; they
Tempt the senses to a kind of play
In which the characters are scenery;
No audience awaits the end but one
Who stares at nothing, and will blindly run
Equally from darkness and from sun.

Some closet all their dead behind one door
And mourn the apparitions they have sown
And rattle on the knob while they implore
Freedom from a jail, which is their own.
Some ageless children murder dreams they gave
Away too soon, and harpies in the grave
Make merrier the birth rites while they rave.

And some invent a calendar that time
Has never witnessed, drawing on the air
Impossible mythologies, and some
Drag through the Odysseys of their despair,
And locked up, finally, in self-made doom,
Wander in their dark from room to room,
Unweaving threads of their unsubtle loom.

And some rehearse a future that the world
Will weed out carelessly: uprooted trees
Flung in a field where winter wind has purled
Along the bough of hope its icicles;
And others, in great pain, will travel far
For false translations of the way they were;
And some will die not knowing who they are.

A STREET WITH CHILDREN

Winter has buried autumn, and the cries
Of children, children on the long blue streets
Fade up into the skies. The telephone wires,
Manuscripts of music where the sparrows sit,
Twang with hidden messages whose music tires
Children looking up into the stars of it.

As daylight fades, the cops and robbers come,
Crying to the pole, Come home, Come home.
A disappearing tear, the single stain
Of the snow man flowing to his icy tomb,
Is blotted in the cinders as the children gain
Tall shadows in the blurry, blue terrain.

Night! Night! A wolf at ankle follows them:
In dreams, their bedrooms drift among the stars
Where blindfold boys play blindman's buff,
And hung from wires, they mediate their wars,
Or turning, their limbs are eaten off—
In dreams, toy wolves are real enough.

Dreamt or perceived, the stars are safe,
And wolves, made up, may be a kind of love.
But children, children wander through the streets
Of woods and cities that are not themselves;
Hunted, they waken, fall unhurt, or weep
To see the wolf in heaven and the stars asleep.

ELEGY FOR MY FATHER

Father, whom I murdered every night but one,
That one, when your death murdered me,
Your body waits within the wasting sod.
Clutching at the straw-face of your God,
Do you remember me, your morbid son,
Curled in a death, all motive unbegun,
Continuum of flesh, who never thought to be
The mourning mirror of your potency?

All you had battled for the nightmare took
Away, as dropping from your eyes, the sea-
Salt tears, with messages that none could read,
Impotent, pellucid, were the final seeds
You sowed. Above you, the white night nurse shook
His head, and, moaning on the moods of luck,
We knew the double-dealing enemy:
From pain you suffered, pain had set you free.

Down from the ceiling, father, circles came:
Angels, perhaps, to bear your soul away.
But tasting the persisting salt of pain,
I think my tears created them, though, in vain,
Like yours, they fell. All losses link: the same
Creature marred us both to stake his claim.
Shutting my eyelids, barring night and day,
I saw, and see, your body borne away.

Two months dead, I wrestle with your name
Whose separate letters make a paltry sum
That is not you. If still you harbor mine,
Think of the house we had in summertime
When in the sea-light every early game
Was played with love and, if death's waters came,
You'd rescue me. How I would take you from,
Now, if I could, its whirling vacuum.

[19]

ADOLESCENT'S SONG

Lopsided love in hotel rooms,
And desperate love, asleep in tombs,
And hour-glass brides and mock bridegrooms
Are not the pure friends that once were we,
O Timothy, Timothy, Timothy.

The mirror man and the paramour,
And broken glass on the slanting floor,
And the midnight punk and the drunken whore
Are not the pure friends that once were we,
O Timothy, Timothy, Timothy.

The vacant loves in apartment halls,
And boys for boys and girls for girls,
And the wilted love that pays the bills
Are not the pure friends that once were we,
O Timothy, Timothy, Timothy.

Goodbye. Bon soir. Farewell. So long.
The singer is parted from his song.
To whom should the singer's song be sung?
Not the pure friend that once you were,
Timothy.

HORROR MOVIE

Dr. Unlikely, we love you so,
You who made the double-headed rabbits grow
From a single hare. Mutation's friend,
Who could have prophecied the end
When the Spider Woman deftly snared the fly
And the monsters strangled in a monstrous kiss
And somebody hissed, "You'll hang for this!"?

Dear Dracula, sleeping on your native soil,
(Any other kind makes him spoil),
How we clapped when you broke the French door
  down
And surprised the bride in the overwrought bed.
Perfectly dressed for lunar research,
Your evening cape added much,
Though the bride, inexplicably dressed in furs,
Was a study in jaded jugulars.

Poor, tortured Leopard Man, you changed your spots
In the debauched village of the Pin-Head Tots;

How we wrung our hands, how we wept
When the eighteenth murder proved inept,
And, caught in the Phosphorous Cave of Sea,
Dangling the last of synthetic flesh,
You said, "There's something wrong with me."

The Wolf Man knew when he prowled at dawn
Beginnings spin a web where endings spawn.
The bat who lived on shaving cream,
A household pet of Dr. Dream,
Unfortunately, maddened by the bedlam,
Turned on the Doc, bit the hand that fed him.

And you, Dr. X, who killed by moonlight,
We loved your scream in the laboratory
When the panel slid and the night was starry
And you threw the inventor in the crocodile pit
(An obscure point: Did he deserve it?)
And you took the gold to Transylvania
Where no one guessed how insane you were.

We thank you for the moral and the mood,
Dear Dr. Cliché, Nurse Platitude.
When we meet again by the Overturned Grave,

Near the Sunken City of the Twisted Mind,
(In *The Son of the Son of Frankenstein*),
Make the blood flow, make the motive muddy:
There's a little death in every body.

A LESSON FROM VAN GOGH

Speechless tree and animal and bird
Vein dreams with meaning, often blurred.
If we could but connect the beast and word!

"The end of life," life callously repeats,
"Is love and its renewal," yet it cheats
Us all in graveyards of eternal streets.

Unharmed by guilt or will, day after day,
The silly fish, performing in the bay,
The simple serpent, lion, pig, and jay,

Are not more separate in each other's sight
Than we who speak—our speech engraves the night
With all the hieroglyphics of delight

That daylight cannot translate. "Take my ear,"
One painter said, who painted out his fear.
Madness has a poetry that comes too near

Truth for comfort: though the mind goes numb,
Thinking of that severance, the deaf and dumb
Communicate by signs, and everyone

Can follow the plain meaning: "Talk to me,"
Van Gogh was saying, "I am not a tree,
A fish, a serpent, lion, pig, or jay."

TRAGEDY

Does a tear fall from the eye
When, falling from great heights,
The body usurps the sky
To die of its appetites?
Do the limbs seek the land
And the lungs a last song
When, burned by cruel wind,
They hurtle headlong?

When to that centre hurled,
Kings have far to fall—
So high, they see the world
Smooth as a round ball—
Perspective takes their wit,
And sceptre, crown, and ring
Must somersault to it,
The whole world darkening.

Those falls from pinnacles
Through miles of royal air

Turn widely in their wheels—
Beggar and priest are there.
All flights of steps may lead
To terror at the top,
The heart begin to bleed
Suddenly without stop,

As when old Caesar's whore
Tore Egypt from her skull,
Or Hamlet's Elsinore
Broke for a lack of will,
Or King Lear on his heath
Invoked the end of breath,
And fools fell out of myth
Into a real death.

All saviors of the city
Are lit by an unknown star;
Love, terror, pity
Walk where they are.
The kings of our great ills
Are dead, yet come to mind
When we fall from small hills
Into the common ground.

A SWIMMER IN THE AIR

That sea we see of surfaces
  Turned upside down would be another world:
A bone shop, soaked in pearl, a dumping-
Ground for rarities, the sea-maws pumping
    Grecian garbage Roman cities hurled
      Seaward westward toward our faces.

  That sea would yield up secret farms,
    Gray-rotted by itself, encrusted thick
With unimaginable wealth, the spoil
Of deaf-mute drownings, the immemorial
    Dead, floating in a blue-green bailiwick
      Of nun-like plants, waving arms.

  That sea will not turn over. See
  In its deepest keep, far from its shallow,
The formal, hidden iceberg, slant, oblique
With pregnancy below, thrust up its peak—
    Like ourselves in the water-beasted wallow,
      Caught in a cellular ecstasy.

[28]

In the same vein, all flesh conceals
Articulation's fishnet, whose thread-bones
(A metaphysic harp from sky to heel)
Hang in the flesh that dangles from the creel
Depending from the weedy Hand that owns
All fishnets and all fishing reels.

His answers breed a further question:
The fingernails of scale a snake will shed
In spring, coil after coil, on moistened clay,
Though similar to the serpent wriggling away,
Are but facsimiles of what we dread.
Testing this, see how the rest shun

Drying memorials to that race
That mined our viewpoint in the Garden,
Whose inching tape maneuvered in the sun
To measure every guilty length of Eden.
Man is an animal that needs a warden
To frighten off the Master's face,

For even an idiot sees a world
No tree or dog would dream of, finds a name
For pain or absence of it, marries love

Of one kind or another. In his grove,
  Insensible fruit trees and wild game
    Grow naturally, though he lies curled,

    The spit and image of our wish,
  Smoking a pipe, with an ice-cold Cola
Clutched in one hand, and the Sunday funnies spread
On both his knees. He'll leave his lurching bed
  To throw hot jazz on an old victrola—
    A far cry from the primal fish

    Whose fine-boned spine our back remembers:
  The river bottoms, and the sea-silt soft
As soup, the mudflats where night crawlers came,
Tempted by the water tops to change the lame
  Arrangements, making of the air a loft
    Fitted to our brackish members,

    And out we clambered, eyeing land,
  Our moist eyes focused on the moron green,
Hot on our backs abnormal dryness, shadow
Forming in the seanets, seaweed into meadow,
  Finally landing at the foot of pine,
    Heavy with salty contraband,

While the birds beautifully beat blue
On erect wings, as magically they soared,
Feathered and efficient, from tallest trees to stake
A claim so ravishing that now we undertake
To map an area we once ignored,
Still exiles from that upper view,

For, mummers of the ocean's Word,
Our dry translations, tidied from the deep,
Bespeak its ancient languages. The salt
Our tears and blood must harbor from its vault
Is shed on every beach-head where we creep,
Part man, dry fish, and wingless bird.

THE SWAN

Darkly at first, through weeds,
The white and youngest swan
Rides on the mirrored lake;
Its lithe, brocaded foot
Barters in reflection
What darkness at the root?

Eye opened on two worlds,
This swan may not perceive
What emblem rides below.
In time's dankest well,
Where eye is infidel,
All images are double.

Weaving from reed to rush,
No shadow of the swan
Is open to caress,
But his one madness,
As neophyte of sun,
Is double beingness.

Lost in the weather of the lake,
Lace-hidden in the water,
Where is the mind's delight?
Oh, which was peerless once,
This braceleted embarker
Or the death of every sense?

When the reeds give way,
This swan is wholly sensual.
What anchorage may weigh
His thinness in the sun?
Fictive on obsidian,
How muscular the swan!

THE GIFT TO BE SIMPLE

Breathing something German at the end,
Which no one understood, he died, a friend,
  Or so he meant to be, to all of us.
  Only the stars defined his radius;
His life, restricted to a wooden house,
Was in his head. He saw a fledgling fall.
  Two times he tried to nest it, but it fell
  Once more, and died; he wandered home again—
  We save so plain a story for great men.
    An angel in ill-fitting sweaters,
    Writing children naïve letters,
  A violin player lacking vanities,
  A giant wit among the homilies—
We have no parallel to that immense
        Intelligence.

But if he were remembered for the Bomb,
As some may well remember him, such a tomb,
  For one who hated violence and ceremony
  Equally, would be a wasted irony.

He flew to formal heavens from his perch,
A scientist become his own research,
   And even if the flames were never gold
   That lapped his body to an ash gone cold,
   Even if his death no trumpets tolled,
     There is enough of myth inside the truth
     To make a monument to fit him with;
   And since the universe is in a jar,
 There is no weeping where his heavens are,
And I would remember, now the world is less,
     His gentleness.

A BOX AT THE OPERA

(For William Meredith)

Into some country where sopranos
Beautifully rage and range, arranging
Echoes beyond the score's intention,
I watched you travel. All was hung there:
Ourselves buoyed up in a box by darkness,
The faint oval glitter across the theatre,
The stage suspended in a gilt rectangle.

Who is to know when music's angel
Arrests its flight and, whirring downward,
Stops to undo its gold illusion?
The music lovers gather at the bar,
The chandeliers assume their mimic brilliance,
The prompter disappears below the stage.

There must be something in old age
That seems like this: a theatre filled
With all that might and could not happen,

More an intermission than an ending,
The audience about to leave its seats,
The actors about to become less real.

And there is someone much too real,
Suffering somewhere in a theatre,
Unknown to the audience or performers,
Whose heart is about to break or stop,
Whose mind is about to close on music,
Whose eyes are about to close on love,

Whose single tear might cancel magic
(Even the magic about that tear),
The marble stairs be brimmed with panic,
The angel dead who brought the music,
And, out in the lobby, a white silk scarf
Hang in the wind like a lost love.

CLICHES FOR PIANO AND ORCHESTRA

(*For Peter Brooks*)

I

That accidental morning,
No garden could deny
Pleasure its misuses;
Cicadas cried bitterly
The language of their briefness.
Then, in the wet eye,
A hopeful desert shook
Its windward, dear oasis,
But I, with a backward look,
Ran from the dread seducers.

II

If I had come to kiss
Cinderella on the bank,
I would know more of this.
I hovered on the brink,
Twirling parent images;

Then, as my heart sank,
The sun sank in the rushes.
I played my water wrist
As a fisherman a line,
But it fell, it fell, all the way down.

III

Plants cannot travel,
Water cannot speak;
The green leaf is rooted,
The blue lake is mute.
(O dark in the dark.)
But if love is a miracle
And I may marvel,
Last night, when I woke,
Plants knew distance
And the water spoke.

IV

By the shore line talk
Of the sweet water lake,
And the rubbery kiss

[39]

In the underwater dark,
By the clutched hair there,
The blue swimmer's lips
Coming near, I swear,
Though the autumn is here,
That the summer took
What it could not take.

V

If trial and error knew
How little in the end
Matters the true-blue
Or the defying, false friend,
How thin the line between
Matter and then none,
The body and the mind,
The grass and the stone,
Then will would be simple
And one decision ample.

VI

As the statue came alive
In the catastrophic purple,
I dug my grave
In the name of the people;
I wrestled with the stone
Till I had no name.
The statue ruled awhile,
Till I struck it down;
Then I could retrieve
My flesh and bone.

VII

Relatives and friends,
A coffin is our end.
Our silhouette is thin
When the worm gets in.
(Black is the bed of green.)
Tie to your skeleton
Therefore your name,
When the wind harps on it
And you are naked to sun,
I will be as you. We will be as one.

THE DUMB SHOW

As many as there are of star and root,
One shifting its position underfoot,
One changing its appearance overhead,
The faces hang their flowers on the dead,

Each dreaming: I am not and am this one;
Sometimes I am the moon, sometimes the sun;
Each tunneling a way up from the dark
Where ghostly busybodies, hard at work

At change, are trying on a thousand things:
The graces of the sea, the rush of wings,
The scalings and the seedpods fleshed on time,
Each trembling on the fact that is its name.

Putting on or taking off in sleep
The many-colored coats of Joseph's sheep,
Some wildly alter hem, some pluck at seam,
The lame becoming lions, the lions tame,

THE DUMB SHOW

Each thinking: What I thought I was I'm not;
I am transformed into the opposite
Of all I seemed to be; I live by strings
Whose ends are fastened onto other beings,

Each making up a kind of makeshift man
Whose tatters are composed, catch as catch can,
Of other selves, now peering out, now in,
Each walking up and down inside his skin;

I feel my heart collapse within its walls,
The humpty dumpty of my ego falls
Into a thousand eggshells of defeat,
For though I hate those strangers when they eat

My heart out, I must also dine on them;
I add their substance to subtract my sum;
I grow into a kind of crippled thing
That cannot crawl or fly or creep or sing

And lies at the bottom of a sandy pit
Where something larger, looking down at it,
Demands its silence. Though it is not me,
Sometimes I think it often tries to be.

If I could only dream myself way up
To the stinging air of freedom at the top,
Rise up from causes I can never reach,
Oh, then, I might say something close to speech.

III

ADVICE TO A TRAVELER

Do not start in a hurricane—
But go in a summer morning's calm
To an anchored boat at the water's rim.
Once in the boat, do not think of *where*;
Dangers enough will beset you there.

Mornings of music that shook you awake
To snow, or a tree like a drawn girl,
You must forget. Do not try to slake
Your thirst too early in the still lake;
Or ask: how shall the heart be whole?

At twilight, when the surface mirrors you,
Its color delicate, its view untrue,
Think: will it last as long as rock,
Long after eyes no sighs renew,
Or pass, indifferently, into dark?

Look up or down in the illusive air:
The lake is shallow at your feet, its glass
Cannot harm you now; nevertheless,
In the sky above you, birds draw
Circles of enormous loneliness.

CRY FROM MONTAUK

This tip is where Long Island ends.
Salt sea surrounds fresh water springs.
Dead lakes reflect dead evenings
As the large hotel reflects dead selves:
From tiers of lighted windows rise
Their prosperous, embarrassed cries.

What glacier fell in lost recoil
To thrust this tip up? On the rocky wheel,
A marvelous flatness flung itself;
The bayberry, crab-like, covers all
The landed sand, and the coastal gull
Remembers its New England.

A Gothic, empty skyscraper,
Sad as a winter roller coaster,
Is the silent policeman of the sea.
Another tower, equally tall,
Guards the farthest edge of all:
The black-white lighthouse barber pole.

Cries of swimmers at the cocktail hour
Drift in disorder from the harbor.
In the formal, recessed patio,
Fireflies play at stop and go;
Severe in starlight, profiles turn
Taut etchings toward the ironed lawn

Where still the natural keeps its vigil.
I hope, some summer night, someone,
Turning his less than empty eyes
To see the lavish emptiness,
Remembers in this starlit grove
Love is the only place we live.

THE HERMIT

Always there is someone who has turned away
From the important mornings and the evening's eye,
Who sits at the top of a tall stairway
Somewhere in the country, or at the edge of slums,
And lives there quietly, day after day,
And does not turn his head to look our way.

What made him leave our ashes and our love?
Did the open sky above the city tempt
His mortal senses to the green, unkempt
Free countryside? And now to disappoint him
The leaves are shy, and the birds
Go about their nests and songs.

Loving the mountains, hating the shore,
Wherever he is, he is not far
From whatever it is that brought him there.
Left in a circle of deserted air,
He draws the edges round him like a tent to hide
The wanderer, traveling inside.

THE HERMIT

His eyes are wild, his island is insane,
We say, and envy secretly his deeper calm.
He calls it home. Perhaps inverted pride,
Pursued in childhood, was his suicide;
Or maybe once, walking in a crowd,
He shuddered at the passion at his side.

Dressed for a battle that has taken place,
Or will never happen, he masks his face
Against the hostile, preferring the alone.
Tuning his armor to the distant guns,
He writes, in a circle, on his shield:
O miseries and appetites of the world.

LETTER TO AN IMAGINARY BRAZIL

(*For Elizabeth Bishop*)

The pink tongues of certain flowers having
Only colloquial names (they are
So tough they might be used for scouring)
Stick out suggestively among green pods,
And the green's tough, too, though it surprises
The fingernail that frees its milk from fibre,
Running a white thread down the hand. One plant's
No menace, but from the plane, one sees
A writhing settlement that hides its danger,
Where snake and puma wrestle on a floor
Of sliding vegetation, and the macaw
May tear a scale off as loud and brilliant
As any virtuoso bending over keys
Of black and white—those colors missing here,
Where all is earth-green, earth-red, earth-brown,
And a sulphurous yellow takes the breath
Away from the breather, Elizabeth.

The waterfall, cruel as a kind of love,
Which, because it moves, is forced to cut
Some life away, is still a version of
The pastoral by being beautiful:
A dynamo that distance turns to song.
The mountain, too, has its deception—
Imagined stillness, though explorers lie
Ironed out among its dark crevasses,
Where nature tries to wrest its forms from darkness:
Twisting, thickening spines and circles
Frightening the mind with a naturalism
That cannot weigh the difference between
A feather and a leaf. To fall asleep at night,
One thinks of nature as a human being:
The mountain a patriarch bending over life,
The waterfall a girl, stranded in a myth,
Whose tears have cut through rock, Elizabeth.

Though what is still may move, and come to grief,
Though what is moving stop, no longer safe,
I see you in your house upon a mountainside,
Lighting the lamps. When you look outside,
There is the room, hung up between the mountains,
Reflected on the other side of glass,

[53]

And, swinging in that double cage of light,
The mind flies out to objects of its love
And finds impenetrable forms and shapes
That you can formulate when you pin down
Each butterfly of thought upon your board.
You'll see, as fine as fern, a single tree
Which, sprouting all its foliage at once,
Will seem to move beneath a microscope
Until each cell is separate to the eye,
Thin-scaled as life upon the width of death,
Who cannot read your poems, Elizabeth.

THE SKIERS

All night we listened to a silent space
Treading on darkness its enormous hall.
From air, as vaporous as moonlight carved
On icebergs sliding from the glacial train,
We took our element: breathed in, breathed out,
Breath was the only sound we ever heard,
Except the hiss of snow.

Time's heirlooms branched beneath us as we sped
Down vacant valleys, as the frozen dead
Piled their neat packages across the ice
And distance made the wounded disappear.
We dropped upon the pastures of pure snow
Into that winter worn explorers know,
Defining worlds with alphabets of snow.

THE SKIERS

Now at the arctic pole, we yearn
For the jungle only, the green rain.
Hope fells the neophytes who cough in snow,
Start for the tropics, and row and row
Through the dead islands of the jaggéd snow.
Where did we wander? Are the branches real
We touch in sleep? Is it spring or fall?

The light evades us when it most defines.
Think of whom we left, gasping among pines.

BERMUDA

Beach house, cabana, bungalow, hotel,
Your walls are weathered by a warped pastel
   Too delicate for sea gulls to detect;
   The run-on blues, the pinkish wrecks
Rattle the air in plaster, coral,
While listless birds attack a wall,
   Adding themselves to the dim graffiti,
   Sometimes obscene, and sometimes witty.

Each morning the landscape seems to be drugged.
Could that quiet bay, overnight, have dragged
   The sea's museum for its salty tortures?
   What we see, from widow's walks and porches,
Is a coastal life of minute reverses:
An orange mothering a withered eel,
   Dead coral hardened to the finest brain,
   And primary colors, after the rain.

The tourist searches for his private symbol,
Vaguely hostile, like a water pistol.

Which is suspicious? Which is correct?
A mirror fragment on the whirling back
Of a Negro dancer, or the plush décor
Of an Empire widow serving tea at four?
Scrawled in chalk in an alleyway:
"Shoeshine 10¢ As Good As Broadway."

Contradiction in terms: a stage set struck
By lightning, the trees, a deaf-mute's joke,
Felt but not heard, its unspoken word
Shouted in a theatre of pastels.
The sea's catastrophes are witticisms,
Heard from a distance, over littered miles.
How can we believe in its total horror,
This hurricane in an ice-cream parlor?

From steeples made of papier-maché
The bell tongues clang, "Relent, Relent"—
As if the sea could condemn or pardon
Itself, the weather, or a crazy garden;
At five o'clock, what the wind is doing
Is semitropical brewing, brewing,
Now calm, now furied, as if it had intent,
And would push its finger through a monument.

AS SUNLIGHT'S FEVER

As sunlight's fever cut across
The sea cove and the rock,
I thought another landscape was
Whispering at my back;
Turning to the slanting wind,
I heard the gulls bark.

But this is another country
And here I have no enemy,
Nothing to do but tarry
By the salt sea or the fresh quarry
Or lie where the slimmest rock divides
Myself from the brimming sea.

Fisherman, though I must remain
Merely a tourist in this town,
Consider me for what I am,
A stranger in a lean time.
Your landscape feeds our loneliness.
The sea belongs to both of us.

FLORIDA

In the unsparing South,
Land of the cotton mouth,
The earth grew green, then black;
The sun, like a heart attack,
Drained juniper and pine
Till twilight stapled down
Their char against the moon
And other lights went on:

Jittery neon rains
Sketching the melted names
Of a thousand glass motels,
Saying the sea's spells
Are profitable and old,
That heaven is never cold
But a tacky, patchwork coast,
Comfortable at a cost.

The tourist "Animal Farms"
Feathered their nests with alms
That flew down from the North,
While giant ferns put forth
Unstinting peals of green,
And, aerialists between
Tree trunks, hairnets of moss
Hung themselves across

The drypoint cypresses.
Everywhere excess
Refurbished its mistake
To make that Spanish fake
Eden a kind of sub-
Suburban country club
Set in an everglade
Of manufactured shade,

Where golfers by the score
Loped to tee and shore,
And all the lives that meant
Only retirement
Teetered to their cars,

To bungalows and bars,
And even the natural seemed
Impermanent and dreamed.

A place where the names of towns
Are prettier than the towns,
Where nothing nervous lives
Except quick primitives:
The serpent of the swamp,
Strange wings around the lamp—
Things from before the Fall
That keep their jungle real.

"Oh, yes, it can enchant.
But it is will I want,"
A Northerner might say,
"Daylight that is less day,
Something with more reserve,
Another kind of love,"
And, loathing the sun's gold,
Race to embrace the cold.

MARINER'S SONG

If you've seen one wave, you've seen them all.
Why don't they come in different colors
Making a rainbow waterfall
In reds and purples, mauves and yellows,
Instead of this green after green sea swell?

What do they do all night at the bottom
But churn their green grains, mud and shells
As furniture, or a fish as a totem,
Wasting the darkness as the sea wills,
Instead of a rainbow, waterfalls?

We cried for color as the boat went over:
The day was blue; the sea was green.
I said, "Love should come out of cover,
Instead of repeating the face, the scene,"—
As wave after greenest wave went over.

[63]

TOURISTS

Cramped like sardines on the Queens, and sedated,
The sittings all first, the roommates mismated,

Three nuns at the table, the waiter a barber,
Then dumped with their luggage at some frumpish
   harbor,

Veering through rapids in a vapid *rapido*
To view the new moon from a ruin on the Lido,

Or a sundown in London from a rundown Mercedes,
Then high-borne to Glyndebourne for Orfeo in
   Hades,

Embarrassed in Paris, in Harris tweed, dying to
Get to the next museum piece that they're flying to,

Finding, in Frankfurt, that one indigestible
Comestible makes them too ill for the festival,

TOURISTS

Footloose in Lucerne, or taking a pub in in
Glasgow or Belfast, or maudlin in Dublin, in-

sensitive, garrulous, querulous, audible,
Drunk in the Dolomites, tuning a portable,

Homesick in Stockholm, or dressed to toboggan
At the wrong time of year in too dear Copenhagen,

Generally being too genial or hostile—
Too grand at the Grand, too old at the Hostel—

Humdrum conundrums, what's to become of them?
Most will come home, but there will be some of them

Subsiding like Lawrence in Florence, or crazily
Ending up tending shop up in Fiesole.

MOUNTAIN AND CLOUDS

Does the hand of God
Sign the accord of cloud?
I see the formal hills
Run with abandoned light,
One out of two worlds made
By the algebra of night.
Does the scene shift by itself,
The green take, shelf by gulf,
Its evening net and spill
All drama on a hill?
Slapdash, a splash of light,
On moored, chromatic dark,
Invites the eyelid's tight
Enclosure to a park
Where everything is green,
Or everything is dark,
Or even the dark is green.

All traffic on a tape
Winds uphill and down.
(I see abandoned hills
Still in a formal light.)
Invention spoils it all:
We cannot leave alone
Contraptions of the Will—
While ruins we create
Clog the mountain gaps,
The cartographer of cloud
Magnificently maps.
The visible reveals
Invisible mystery;
And the hand of God is green,
If it is the hand of God;
If it moves at all, it moves
According to a cloud.

EXPLORERS

Though Circe's music lured Ulysses on,
Less famous instances of silences
Have worked an equal magic: Coming down
Rivers, crossing seas, in desert spaces,
There were a thousand nights when no one spoke
And the stars dipped away in the cold dark.

The weary animals, afraid of wind
On sand, their legs as delicate as grass,
Fed on what vegetation came to hand,
While sailors stoked the ocean's underpass
Miles away, for treasure or for truth,
And heard the same wind discharge its wrath.

And there was fact, and there was magic: trees
That spun around or fought or stood stock-still,
A myth of fishes and a book of leaves,
And setting forth to find the sacred hill,
Where mind and body parted in their dread,
And the left hand dreamt, and the right hand did.

EXPLORERS

What shores receded as they sighted land!
The bellied sails embarked, splendid of motion,
To lay their wings upon the sea, unmanned
Ambassadors of dry rot to the ocean.
Young tyrants, in a fever, shook with cold,
Before they tumbled down, and then grew old.

And it is all the same. The king, falling,
Rises in new splendor but to fall again;
His jealous princeling, who can kill a king,
Is waiting in the wings, and then walks on,
Whose disputatious arms retake the field
While dead kings sift the layers of the world.

And those who passionately would not see
That time and silence take what they would have,
In fear, or love, have sought the mystery
Of what lay menacing beyond the grave,
As once, in Florida, water would not sing
When Ponce de Leon babbled at the spring.

VENICE

Its wingéd lion stands up straight to hide
The source of pain: the reign of the unnatural.
One cannot tell how really false the real is.
One cannot tell how real the really false is.
Seen in one light, we apprehend the Beautiful:
The thinnest minarets of lattice lacework
Tangibly recovered from the hardest natural
Elements command our endless homage:
One doorway makes our human lives seem trivial.
In yet another light, a scabrous limb of Venus,
Dangling in rank water, rots to golden bone—
The swank and stink of the imagination
Beautifully gone bad. Its waterways re-weave
The only city that has seen itself
Reflected in the mirror of its very eye,
Made-up, each century, in vain for views
No one can now remember. How the painters lie,
Taken altogether, in their fabrication!
Even the Adriatic, static in its green,
Evokes no known sea. From the campanile,

One sees, face down, a short, ceramic fish
Glittering its red-tiled scales below.
Exquisite emphases and subtle losses
Make up its tide. For power, four bronze horses,
Brought from Byzantium, outpace the sun.
Dwindling to our shadows in outside salons
Where orchestras of afternoon rehearse our evening,
We sound the very history of fear we felt
Through all the shorter histories of fear we feel.
Is it true, we think, our sorry otherness
Is to fall in love with beasts whose beauty ruins us?
Those beasts are everywhere, though Venice says
Lions to be golden must be painted gold.

LOCAL PLACES

The song you sang you will not sing again,
Floating in the spring to all your local places,
Lured by archaic senses to the wood
To watch the frog jump from the mossy rock,
To listen to the stream's small talk at dark,
Or to feel the springy pine-floor where you walk—
If your green secrecies were such as these,
The mystery is now in other trees.

If, in the desert, where the cactus dryly,
Leniently allows its classic bloom
To perfume aridness, you searched for water,
And saw, at night, the scalp of sand begin
To ripple like the sea, as though the moon
Had tides to time those waves of light's illusion,
The rock that spilled so softly from your hand
Is now ten thousand other grains of sand.

If you lay down beside the breathing ocean,
Whose lung is never still, whose motion pulls

A night-net over sleep, you knew the way
It lulled the dreamer toward his vision, how
Drowned mariners turned over in its slough,
Green-eyed among the weeds. You see it now
A less than visionary sea, and feel
Only its blue surfaces were ever real.

Or if you were born to naked flatness
Of rock, or rock that twisted up in mountains,
The jagged risers stonily ascending,
And bent down once to see the mica's tight,
Flat scales of silver, layered in the granite,
And kept one scale to be your jewel at night,
Another sliver now breaks light; its gleam
Is similar to yours, yet not the same.

Once history has used your single name,
Your face is one time will not see again.
Into such a din is every singer born,
The general music mutes the single horn.
The lights in the small houses, one by one,
Go out, foundations topple slowly down—
The tree, the sand, the water, and the stone,
What songs they sing they always sing again.

[73]

IV

KING MIDAS

I · THE KING'S SPEECH

My food was pallid till I heard it ring
Against fine china. Every blessed thing
I touch becomes a work of art that baits
Its goldsmith's appetite: My bread's too rich,
My butter much too golden, and my meat
A nugget on my plate, as cold as ice;
Fresh water in my throat turns precious there,
Where every drop becomes a millionaire.

My hands leak gold into the flower's mouth,
Whose lips in tiers of rigid foliage
Make false what flowers are supposed to be.
I did not know I loved their warring thorns
Until they flowered into spikes so hard
My blood made obdurate the rose's stem.
My God was generous. But when I bleed,
It clogs the rosebed and cements the seed.

[77]

My dog was truly witty while he breathed.
I saw the tiny hairs upon his skin
Grow like a lion's into golden down.
I plucked them by the handfuls off of him,
And, now he is pure profit, my sculpturing
Might make a King go mad, for it was I
Who made those lively muscles stiffly pose—
This jaundice is relentless, and it grows.

I hate the glint of stars, the shine of wheat,
And when I walk, the tracings of my feet
Are affluent and litter where I go
With money that I sweat. I bank the slow
Gold-leaf of everything and, in my park,
A darkness shimmers that is not the dark,
A daylight glitters that is not the day—
All things are much less darling gilt this way.

Princess, come no closer; my tempered kiss,
Though it is royal still, will make you this
Or that kind of a statue. And my Queen,
Be armed against this gold paralysis,
Or you will starve and thinly bed alone,

And when you dream, a gold mine in your brain
Will have both eyes release their golden ore
And cry for tears they could not cry before.

I would be nothing but the dirt made loud,
A clay that ripples with the worm, decay
In ripeness of the weeds, a timid sun,
Or oppositely be entirely cloud,
Absolved of matter, dissolving in the rain.
Before gold kills me as it kills all men,
Dear Dionysus, give me back again
Ten fingertips that leave the world alone.

II · THE QUEEN'S SONG

The palace clocks are stiff as coats of mail.
Time stopped; he flicked it with his fingernail.
O he was mine before he was a mine
      Of gold.

Time's twelve cold sentinels so grimly still
No longer chime their golden interval.
O he was love before he was the love
      Of gold.

What treasurer is this, come to my bed,
Whose suppleness is now a golden rod?
O he was King before he was the King
      Of gold.

III · THE PRINCESS' SPEECH

I praise the bird, the river, and the tree.
One flies, one flows, and one has made me see
That, standing still, the world is turning me.

I cannot fly. Birds carry in the morn.
I cannot flow. A river bed is born.
I grow. My leaves are green, and gold, and torn.

Divided into two, I am a tree.
The branches are too high for me to see,
The roots too hidden from reality.

They say that veins of gold lie underground.
Beware, explorers, of the spoil you find:
Though you sail back and forth, you sail around.

The laurel grows upon the laurel tree.
Apollo plucked the string of mystery
And made a golden echo in the sea.

IV · THE QUEEN'S SPEECH

May every child of mine be barren, golden!
May every beast become a golden swine!
Here is a list, O gardeners and huntsmen,
Of what to kill and what to leave alone:
All natural things must go excepting those
That are by nature golden. Whatever grows
The King's touchy color let live, but close
Your nets upon the pink and crimson rose.

But I will save one rose tree in this pot
That I may gaze at it, and when he's not
About, I'll look and look till light is gone

At flower, petal, stem, and leaf. And then,
I'll ponder how a King became a fool!
Long live King Midas! And the Golden Rule!

V · THE HUNTSMAN'S SONG, THE GARDENER'S REFRAIN

Is it the hawk or hare,
Blindly alive to feed,
The daylight rises for?
I have seen both bleed,
Yellow and dead.

Is it the clang of war
I waken to instead
Of the hunt as heretofore?
That shot was in my head,
Yellow and dead.

The quarry goes before.
The hunter must be fed.

I know the huntsman's lore.
I know that blood is red,
Yellow and dead.

Nature cannot bear
To gild its marriage bed
With gold that is not there.
The golden goose is dead,
Yellow and dead.

VI · ADDRESS BY DIONYSUS

There is no meekness in my sun.
It is more dazzling than the one
You cannot look at, Midas. Run
   This way or that, it follows you,
   And is indifferent to the view.

A king especially must live
Without a God's prerogative.
We take, for every gift we give,
   Two back. Your gold made you a fool.
   Now you grow wise, but in my school.

[83]

There is a lesson children learn:
You reach your hand out, and you burn.
It is no lesson kings can spurn.
   Mine is a cruel curriculum
   Not fit for the powerless or dumb.

Go to the river. Dip your hand
Into its silver rumblings. Stand
Still while the precious contraband
   You glitter with flows from your skin
   Till water sucks away your sin.

It is through will, and only will,
Pleasure unearths the sensual.
The Gods grind error in a mill
   Whose gold wheels turn all costly wit
   Into its dreaded opposite.

VII · THE PRINCESS' SONG

See how they love me,
Green leaf, gold grass,
Swearing my blue wrists
Tick and are timeless.

See how it woos me,
Old sea, blue sea,
Curving a half moon
Round to surround me.

See how it wants me,
High sky, blue sky,
Letting the light be
Kindled to warm me.

Yet you rebuke me,
O love, love I
Only pursue. See
How they love me!

VIII · THE KING'S SONG

What I loved most most moved me.
Tell me, soul, where now your motion is.
Looking back, I look on Orpheus,
Who, looking back, looked on Eurydice.

His voice is distant as the shelled sea.
She, underground, is where no music is.
They moved me most who loved me.
Tell me, flesh, where now your motion is.

I, an ancient King, walk blindly.
I break on pleasure where no pleasure is.
Looking back, I look on Orpheus,
Who, looking back, looked on Eurydice.

IX · DIONYSUS' SONG

Midas in the street
Makes statues out of men.
When man and money meet,
Beware! The worst is then.

Beware! The worst is then.

[86]

When animal and angel
Meet on a common ground,
And elegance is natural,
Nothing is so profound.

Nothing is so profound.

X · THE KING TO THE PRINCESS, AT THE RIVER BANK

My daughter, the river flows down to the sea.
All things begin in its rich nursery.
If you should shed a tear, shed it for me.

Remember me for this: if you should gain
What men most wish for, give it back again,
Before the Gods transform it into pain.

Stay here beside me while I dip my hand
Into the cold river. Until water end,
Pactolus, from this day, runs golden sand.

BURNING LOVE LETTERS

I

Fire that cancels all that is
Devours paper and pen
And makes of the heart's histories
A cold hearth warm again.
It could as well consume a branch,
Blank paper or black coal
That now, in ashy avalanche,
Scatters the heart whole.

II

What words led to the end of words?
Coldly, all separate sighs
Shiver in flame, flying upwards,
Merged into burnt lies.
In somersaults of light, words burn
To nothingness, then roll
In dead scrolls, delicate as fern,
Or hiss like a waterfall.

III

From partial feast to total fast,
From object to mirage,
An animal that cannot last
Appears in fire's cage:
Love's crazy dog in a cold sweat,
Far from its neighborhood,
Circles the puzzle of regret,
On fire in the wood.

IV

Love's ashes lie and will not rise
As fire dies to a black sun
And makes of the heart's histories
A warm hearth cold again.
Cremation's scattered dust confronts
Dead vision, and in these
Ashes I write your name once,
Bending on cold knees.

SONG

The air is the only
Lonely bearer
Of the one breath
Of love's wayfarer.
The sea's too wet
To forgive. Forget
Its salty ranges:
Change changes.

But sing flesh
Sinew and bone
And mostly blood,
The fine wood
In which we hive
The dead and alive,
The hollow vein
And love's rain.

THE FALLS OF LOVE

I

I know so many stories marred by love,
Tales told by bitter voices in the dark:
Those who stand before the open window
Afraid to see their hands that might let go;
And other hands that count departed loves,
Ten icicles inside a pair of gloves.

II

What faces tell its crooked narrative
Make everywhere their small appearances:
Dried flags of warning that commemorate
A feast that failed, or fasts that failure fed;
Or worse, young faces that too soon reveal
How eyes may witness what they cannot feel.

III

Only lovers rest in summer's grove,
Warm in the hollow belly of the hill.
They feel the lizard's slowness, see the sea
The mother of desire, and become the tree
They shelter under. As those leaves of skin
Burn, they burn to say: Love, stay, till autumn.

IV

A winter comes where love will never live:
In darkened windows, shadowed heads receive
Night sounds that hold affection in their strings,
And harp on the harpings of themselves to give
Cold strumming warm illusion, and to stir
False, five-fold music in the listener.

V

A body without love is in its grave.
There is a still life that all sleepers dread
That only love can motion from the dead.

Though he walk upright where green grasses wave,
He wears a little earth upon his head
Who shuns the marriage for the single bed.

VI

They rise up shining who have love to give;
Who give love freely may all things receive.
Though streams they cross can never be the same,
They know the waters of the earth are one;
They see the waking face inside the dream
Who know the variations are the theme.

VII

I know so many stories marred by love,
What faces tell its crooked narrative.
Only lovers rest in summer's grove;
A winter comes where love will never live.
A body without love is in its grave—
They rise up shining who have love to give.

IF YOU CAN

Countryman, tell me if you can,
When your fist rounds the tender corn
And shakes the minerals of the grain,
If one can live by bread alone.

For I have loved

Fisherman, tell me if you can,
When your scarred, glinting catch is slain
And pitted on the rock, if then
The diamonds of the sea are torn.

For I have loved
But not loved well

Physician, tell me if you can,
When you part wires in the skin
And open up the bank of bone,
Is the blood sea or is it sun?

For I have loved
But not loved well
And cannot tell

And you I walk on, if you can,
Tell me if you are snow or moon,
Or rise by some invention
Into a garden out of stone.

For I have loved
But not loved well,
If I have loved
At all.

WATERWALL BLUES

I gnarled me where the spinster tree
Unwound its green hosanna
And built its sorrow, leaf by knee,
A lachrymal cabana.

The selfsame night I cracked my cowl,
Unwound myself with Anna;
Speech by speech and howl by howl,
O don't you cry Susanna!

I left my childhood sadness near
The winder of blue water,
Walking in the windmill year
With his summer daughter.

That very night I spoke my piece,
Unwound my heigh-ho merry,
Started my newfangledness
Across her downtown ferry.

But when my halfway laughing gulls
Despair the death of her,
Dumb sorrow rides the same old hulls
With his mad mariner.

THE TRUTH ABOUT LOVE

It seems to have traveled mostly at night,
Supremely ironic, lighting fires,
Laying golden eggs in the midst of squalor,
Its outer garments, in the latest version,
Sumptuous, its linens more than shoddy,
Drunk, moreover, at a seedy party
The discriminating shunned, and, later, bawdy
In a run-down neighborhood, with whores and sailors
Chosen as companions while the queen went needy.
Now that everything about it is known,
Why does it come up purple or threadbare,
Thrashing all its sunsets in a fit of pique,
Or stripped, in the seamiest hayloft, ready
To repeat dull anecdotes the millionth time,
Its poise unquestionable, its voice unsteady?
It is brilliant, androgynous, and stultifying
With its threats and tears, dissembling always
Its mad obsession with the blurred distinction.
And yet who else
Is so elementary and badly needed

That fifty cultures rise at the merest rumor
Of its presence, and, finally, punctually fall
Whenever it departs, as if on schedule?
Interviewed, Monday, in the city dump,
Which turned, by magic, into a hotel tower,
Shedding poems and paintings for its bath
(It takes ten centuries of running water
To wash it clean), it then emerged, all dirty
Again, in a costume of ferocious splendor,
A hat some milliner in old Vienna
Sweated over, its pumps exchanged for sneakers,
And raced across the city, breaking records,
Just to prove its powers of endurance.
It lies down anywhere, and loves the country,
But is so unassuming it can even flourish
Beneath electric signs and in railroad stations
It goes to for the summer, estivating,
It says, near fountains that escape our notice,
And comes back in the fall, its ribbons flying,
Wheeling through the leaves, singing all the voices
Of every opera in the repertoire
Plus one no one has ever dreamed of writing.

Going about its gigantic business,
It masks itself as any shape or hope,
Appearing as a vicious telephone call,
Or a flat, disturbing prophet in an envelope.
It praises calmness but adores upheaval,
Is most to be desired when it apes composure,
And much to be distrusted when it boasts it has
The only fingerprint that can be changed at will.

A SONG STRUCK FROM THE RECORDS

Dear fairy Godmother, hold back
    Your magic transformation;
I see a coming cul-de-sac
    In rising above my station.
I know my clothes are awful, my
    Room a mess, but then,
At least I'm not surrounded by
    Secret service men.
I fear the Prince's hunting lodge,
    I fear, my dear, his mother;
Frankly, I hate the whole hodgepodge,
    And the infernal bother.

No Prince falls short of the ideal
    Except on close inspection,
And royal houses, once they're real,
    Reveal some imperfection:
The widest moat, so crystal clear
    Today, becomes tomorrow

A muddy ditch with scummed veneer,
  Incredibly more narrow.
I'd be, should you invoke your wand,
  More sinned against than sinning,
And sadder at the happy end
  Than at the sad beginning.

RAIN

Dear, on a day of dumb rain,
When cats sleep and trees grow,
And, outside the windowpane,
Imaginary fish flow,
We, as lovers, lace our arms
Securely round each other's back,
Hoping to stave off lightning's harm,
To counter thunder's crack.

Then pleasure is as easy as
The body's closeness, and the mind's;
There is a kind of love that has
Them separate, but body finds
Body too tasteless without thought,
And lovers feel, when face to face,
That mere intellect falls short,
Short of an embrace.

Dwindling, the slim rain makes us seem
As green as any world that grows;
Intransitive in sleep, we dream
Ourselves curled tightly as the rose,
Whose bud we cannot praise too much:
This is the start of every song
That no philosophy can touch—
And only the dead are wrong.

SMALL ELEGY

In the smart room where Lennie lies,
French draperies are too silk for eyes
That like their hangings plain, like their ties
Thin-striped. Lennie will no more arise

And go now where the cocktail shakers shake
Their crystal energies and pianists fake
Some lovelorn valentines and, on the make,
Mirrored faces join, and part, and break.

And since those wretched limbs, not custom-made
But real, and common, in a last charade
Crumble into peace, who's to parade
Up Fifth and down with all his tricks of trade?

The chandelier, the chiffonier, the waste
By-products of the golden calf, Good Taste,
Surround his body. To his Never-Faced-
Reality, gentlemen, a final toast!

Damn it, he had good taste! That's all he had.
He knew the nearly-good from the not-quite-bad.
Lennie wore the first vest made of plaid.
Lennie gave it up when it became a fad.

Goodbye, Lennie—fad, plaid, and Madras!
May artificial angels and high brass
Proclaim a high-fidelity Mass
When you step from, and into glass.

THE FEAST

The lies we have to tell
Become unforgettable,
And the loves, oh, the loves
That a sick fervor proves
Every day more exhausted,
Thinner and more wasted,
Come to no known end,
Whichever way they wind.
And two, locked in a room,
Consume that gray, grim
Feast of parenthood,
Guilt, their one food.

A MARRIAGE

O hardly out of hate,
He flew down flights of stairs
  To where she lay;
  Too tender to berate
    His long delay,
  She fell in love with flight.

He fell in love with her,
Who'd counted all the stares
  That marked his way.
  A tardy traveler
    In love with time,
  He heard the clocks whir.

She heard the cocks wake
Pastel and country towns.
  He loved the city,
  Dangerous as a snake,
    In love with him.
  She heard his heart break.

He saw her broken eyes
Too many years too late
  To make them whole;
  He found, to his surprise,
    It was himself
  Who dammed those pretty eyes.

She pitied pity. Wise
Too late, she thought she'd take
  To dressing up
  In any old disguise
    To keep from him
  Their happiness of lies.

Though happy for a time,
He came to know too soon
  The cost of tears
  Unshed. He aped her crime
    For years. For years,
  They lived a double shame.

And they could never give
Enough to get away
From where they hid,
And both took to the grave
The harm they, did,
Their necessary love.

CHALK FROM EDEN

Doctrine has wound of lovers' limbs
A sulphurous wreath of antonyms,
And strung its gnomes of hell and damn
On wiry thoughts throughout all time,
And taken a stick to the naked couple,
Cursing the moonlight, the river bend,
Music, and dark—and the world goes round.

For virgins will come, all green thumb,
Into the garden of their martyrdom,
And dilly-dally in the orchard air,
And say to holy doctrine, "Less we care
For the black commandments of your lasting scruple
Than we do for a dancer who is supple;
Hell is not heaven, and go to the devil."

And time and again, in every season,,
Love will awake from the dream of reason,
And young and old will walk in their park,
And spin in their skins from light to dark.
The sheets of time have a common wrinkle,
For youngsters will take their flaking chalk
And write of love on wall and sidewalk.

THE VIEW MINUS ONE

We lay where we could take the sun.
  From eyesight's eminence on that high roof
The city angled down; when I could look,
I saw a courtyard and ailanthus tree.
  A moth whose single day was spent
On water paper wings had fluttered down
A cranny where the sun had feathered him;
Instinctive wings on my bare skin
  Their sad and final supper took.

Though not quite naked either was
  (As bathers for the sea dress, we for sun)
The moth's suggestion was a naked one:
Our skin, a groaning board for him,
  Was edible as wool; in dining there,
Both skins for cloths dissembled were;
By slow unweaving of our sunlit clothes
His wish uncovered what we could not choose
  To ravel into dusty air.

The moth unwound us till our round
   And raveled substance (and unraveled) twined
In that dead wedding. Was the tree real coin,
As the light on a staircase of itself walked up
   The edges of the evening? If the tree could sup,
As the moth did, on fare so alien,
Our marriage bed was merely mirrored green,
Our vows, moth-eaten, mere reflection
   Of an insect and ailanthus scene.

I lie in sunlight where we once lay down.
   Mere moth, long since its flying linen
Leveled into dust, has flown—and you
Are gone. O lost subtraction from the view,
   In wildness, under sunlight, I would kiss
Again, again, again, your nakedness.
Now panic has its rooftop all alone,
For square, hot, real, below,
   Insect traffic stops to go.

THE LIE

Some bloodied sea-bird's hovering decay
Assails us where we lie, and lie
To make that symbol go away,
To mock the true north of the eye.
But lie to me, lie next to me;
The world is an infirmity.

Too much of sun's been said, too much
Of sea, and of the lover's touch,
Whole volumes that old men debauch.
But we, at the sea's edge curled,
Hurl back their bloody world.
Lie to me, lie next to me,

For there is nothing here to see
But the mirror of ourselves, the day,
Clear with the odors of the sea.
Lie to me. And lie to me.

LIGHT AND DARK

Your eyelash is a shade
For my most lovely luminary;
    Open, its transitory,
Finely-pronged, reverse cascade

    Reveals the ambushed white
Liquid sky whose oval ground
    Backs the colored round
That is my circle of delight,

    As dazzling as the sea,
When, swimming out beyond my height,
    I dive, from toppling light,
Down to the deepest dark can be.

    And there are other lights:
When the electric sky ignites
    Windows on heights, or sleights
Of hand—sunrise and sunset kites

Vanishing up and up
Beyond what vision understands,
    Like moonlight on my hands,
Or the spectrum in a waterdrop.

    When fireworks go off,
Scribbling flowers on the sky,
    Though they streak up high,
They never go quite high enough,

    For darkness settles down
Again, and then too soon the black
    Crown above me is back,
And I walk slowly in to town,

    Moved by I know not what.
Is it not that the flash has shown
    Me, standing alone,
How huge the dark is I forgot?

    And I forget again,
Seeing those two loved brilliancies
    Dredge up from subtle seas
The sunken fragments of the sun,

Or the colorless moon—
Whose changing luminosity
    Does and undoes the sea—
Ballooning out, or thin pontoon.

    But it is starlight, surely,
That is most like those eyes I love
    When stars hang where they hive
To make night late and morning early;

    As distances debar
From touch those lights that, moving near,
    Move us more and more—
Alight, the dark is where you are.

VI

PINE

Its fringy needles stiff
As horsehair, glaucous, fine,
Form a kind of leaf;
Each leaf's a smaller branch,
Each branch a smaller tree,
The whole scaled to the inch,
The inch to infinity.
And so pine is what Plato
Might deem the universal
Universal, for
It is that metaphor
With roots in the divine:
The great in the small design.

A pair of winged seeds—
Each like a butterfly
With wings at the vertical,
Folded, at rest—can fly
Out over the world
And haul up in the sun

PINE

The bud and bone of pine.
Ecclesiastical,
Beautiful short or tall,
We cut it down. And yet,
Revenge is in its wit:
When we are cased in it,
There's pine to every fit.

ROUNDS

I

Tented against the glare
Of sunlight overhead,
The leaves screen the heat,
And what might devil air
Angelically is bred,
By coolness and by fleet
Shutters everywhere,
To summer's true bed:
The greenness of retreat.

We follow freshness where
The spring winds led,
And climb to heaven's seat
Up an endless stair
To green rooms just ahead
On persevering feet;
Opening each door,
We find, refurbishèd,
New worlds complete.

How meagre was the spare
Landscape we have shed!
How rare the bird's sweet
Whistle, full and clear,
That sings of the unsaid,
Above the green sheet
Spread to cover bare
Earth and the new dead!
Angelic and elite

Heiresses of air,
We feel you overhead,
And though we may not greet
You equally, our share
Is half the marriage bed
We come to on young feet
To wed you everywhere,
Our flesh no longer lead.
Lightly your wings beat.

II

Fire and leaf are kin
When the leaves blow away
And the bitter season reigns.
The sky erases green
From one more tree each day
Till only the pale stains
Of summers that have been
Fade in the sun's ray.
We make of these remains

A fire for within:
Blade after blade of hay,
Deserts of dry grains,
Are stored within the bin
Of the color-wheeling tree.
Astringent in our veins,
Thin life, a pricking pin.
Bleeds the summer lie
Only the blood retains.

Pinion and horizon
Rise on a changed day
When beasts of weathervanes,
Turning their burnt tin,
Spin against the sky.
Holding the long reins
That fire in the sun,
Flame, like a runaway,
Races the long rains

Whose seasonable din
Shatters the still day
Where false summer feigns
Old miracles of sun.
In mirrors of new gray,
The colorless remains
Of leaves, flame or green,
Hang or blow away
Till the kindling wanes.

III

The season of Alas
Winters in the sky;
The ground is white with snow.
What archeries of glass
Blind the naked eye,
Illusionary arrow!
Its target is a guess:
We aim at the bull's eye,
Half light, half shadow.

Draughtsmanship is less
Than color to the eye
In love with summer's show.
A season of duress
Paints a rare, wry
Canvas. Eyes that know
Shun the obvious:
There is no subtlety
Like white and its dumb show.

A museum of undress,
What costumes it could try
It's happy to forego.
It is not sounding brass:
The bony and the spry
Plucked arpeggio
Can nakedly compress
Music to one sigh,
Mocking the piano.

Everything made less
Itself is winter's way:
The lowest trees bow low
To let the wind pass,
Rummaging the dry
Snow that sifts below
Their naked likenesses,
Cold as the cold sky,
Blind with heavy snow.

IV

Black and white go down.
Spring's petals spring,
One by one, to life;
Pink, or vermilion,
Upon the branch's sling
Is born and is brief.
A longing for the sun
Stretches along the limb
And hangs the shapely leaf.

A pink and green clown
Tumbles in the ring;
We see with disbelief
A comic in a gown
From sterile twigs wring
The greenest green sheaf
Of flowers under the sun,
And the sun itself strung
On flower and on leaf.

Now who can disown
The new-born changeling?
The woods and fields are rife
With grinning green;
And should the bee sting
Young flesh unsafe,
There's honey in the comb,
More honey coming
To tongues that have enough.

Angels, earth has shown
Its heart to be too big:
Standing in spring we sniff
A newness all our own,
And though its whirligig
Can spin us through one life,
And only one, on loan,
We dance a joyous jig
On limbs soon stiff.

A PORTRAIT

(*For Gertrude Buckman*)

Yes, she craves diminutive things:
The sea shell and the carousel
Obliquely seen through an opera glass,
And the faint colors on the wind that pass—
Not the red of the loud bell,
But the shadow echoed in the well.

Yes, she is aware of innuendo,
The splendid underscoring of these things;
A skull is therefore Mexico,
And the humming bird sings
Loudest. Not the jay, or the gull,
But the ultimate infinitesimal.

Yes, she believes in overtones:
The statues alive at twilight,
Not the word said, but the word unspoken,
Not the gift, but the token.
To her, a pin-point instant star
Is the history of all incredible light.

ROMANTIC LOVE: A FOOTNOTE

The ill-used sea
And its ancient laundry
Tosses up a dirty
Wash or two,
Which puts in question
Thoughts of eternity:
Grapefruit and tar
Are not incredible blue.

Somebody ought to raise
A banner for
A possible life,
A dirty sea floor,
The general seediness
Of all good things
That do not glide like swans
Or sit like kings.

UNDERWOOD

From the thin slats of the Venetian blinds
The sun has plucked a sudden metaphor:
A harp of light, reflected on the floor,
Disorients the chair and desk and door.
Those much too delicate hands still tapping
The Underwood seem now Hindu dancers
Or five or ten young Balinese children
Hopping up and down in a clearing where
The striped light scrapes through bamboo seedlings
And moves from skinny shade to thin veneer
And changes as the harp of light is changing
Its twanging image on the office floor,
Being so remarkably the blinding heir
Of something that is not, and yet is, there.

Once I watched at the water cooler
A face bent over the jet-thin water:
The iris of the bent eye changed its color
As if the water jet had stained it green;
I saw the animal head's slight shudder,

Lifted from the surface of that running stream.
Tall branches then grew green in the hallway,
Arching above a green-ferned pathway;
A screen of green leaves hung in the doorway.
Was that a mirror where I saw the beaked birds,
The sluggish coffin of the alligator,
The monkeys climbing up the sunlit tree trunks?
Or did imagination, in that corridor,
Create, like the harp, its sudden metaphor?

Inside that drawer, among the blotters, folders,
Memos, carbons, pencils, papers,
Is the youngest animal of all awaking
In that coarse nest where he's been sleeping?
If I should reach into that dangerous drawer,
What singular teeth might pierce my skin?
Or if he should leap, should I then kill him,
And watch, where the harp had set its lightness,
The marvelous animal blood go thin?

WINTER'S END

Once in a wood at winter's end,
The withered sun, becoming young,
Turned the white silence into sound:
Bird after bird rose up in song.
The skeletons of snow-blocked trees
Linked thinning shadows here and there,
And those made mummy by the freeze
Spangled their mirrors on cold air.
Whether they moved—perhaps they spun,
Caught in a new but known delight—
Was hard to tell, since shade and sun
Mingled to hear the birds recite.
No body of this sound I saw,
So glassed and shining was the world
That swung on a sun-and-ice seesaw
And fought to have its leaves unfurled.
Hanging its harvest in between
Two worlds, one lost, one yet to come,
The wood's remoteness, like a drum,
Beat the oncoming season in.

Then every snow bird on white wings
Became its tropic counterpart,
And, in a renaissance of rings,
I saw the heart of summer start.

ELIZABETHAN TRAGEDY: A FOOTNOTE

That prudent Prince who ends Shakespearian plays
And wanders in to tell us how we wasted time
To hate or fall in love or be deranged
Would, three hours earlier, have ruined the play.
And so experience is, after all,
The heart of the matter. Even chatter
And babbling, or scenes in the worst of love affairs,
Like tears or throwing things or being pushed down-
    stairs
Have value in the long run. Caution has its place.
Premeditation, though, I think, when face to face
With *sturm und drang* can never win the race.
Although the Prince is on the angels' side,
What got him there is wholesale homicide.

SKIN AND BONE

The wick burns down the length
Of its cold paraffin
Till the burnt string's strength
Sputters, and is gone;

And if you have not seen
The spider in his web
Make of that silk machine
A jail where small things ebb,

You cannot know I mean
The skin around the bone.

The heavy leaves of blight
Curl inward and come down;
It is the moth of light
The darkness tumbles down;

SKIN AND BONE

And if you cannot see
The crab's dry rattling legs
Turn over, claw the sky,
And wither to the dregs,

You cannot know I mean
The skin around the bone.

The string stands for the nerve,
The web stands for the brain,
The wing for the eyelid's curve,
The leaf stands for the skin,

But the claw is appetite
That feeds on that heart each night
You cannot know. I mean
The skin around the bone.

AROUND THE FISH: AFTER PAUL KLEE

I

The mind from nature, divorced by love,
Stunned into being by the running wave,
Swims backward always. Around the fish,
Unreasoning sensation made a wish:
Parsley, persevering in a tree,
Maturely withers in the alchemy
Of elms and willows. So with us,
The elementary is most serious.

II

Wishing, the Fisher King sat down.
Bait was his body, but his catch a crown!
Incarnate fish food rose again,
Hooked to the level of his flawless line;
The sea stirred; sunlight's mica hurled

Aroma of the fish around the world;
Darwin breathed it on another shore,
Gasping the less than liquid air.

III

Swimmers, crying in the undertow,
A water blinds us where we go;
The whirlpool of the inner eye
Has wet ambitions, casts its fly
On sightless water; baited, fed,
Its fishing pole hangs by a thread.
But Christ lies on the blue plate, still.
The spawnless salmon strike to kill!

SALT–WATER TAFFY

Their long skirts stiffened by the salty air
Waved at the sea's edge to those bathing;
High cries drowned out the ocean's roar
When, accidentally, they went wading.

The sweet sun sieved vague afternoons.
The beach was a waste of lace, and sandy.
Raspberry sherbet went down in spoons
To prove the summer was a box of candy.

The boardwalk, tigered, sun by shadow,
Whirled them across its thin bars daily;
Bracken and seaweed, but no meadow,
Veered with the wind, wailing palely.

Noons, under strict shade, sad they sat,
Wishing the day's loose sails would tighten;
Taffy was all they doted on, yet
Love might have come at Coney, Brighton.

SALT-WATER TAFFY

Where are they now, those hour-glass girls
Who walked the boards at Atlantic City
Eating their sticks of salt-water taffy,
To whom the summer was a box of candy?

THE WIND IS ROUND

Season into season, as the weathers go,
The wind weighs roses as it swings the snow.
As spring contains its fall, the rose its thorn,
The eye has its nothingness. Death is born.

The sleeping window where the frost star holds,
Holds window boxes; folded leaves unfold,
Green from ice artifice. See the seed
Flung to the consequences of the weed!

The eye, though shut, can dream of any weather:
Opiate sky, or forsythia feather.
All drowsy combinations sift behind
Its opalescence, though the opal, blind,

Sees all views black. So light that's white
Is really rainbow-colored, and all night
The far stars shine. If we could see by day,
They'd hang there, dazzling, in the same array.

THE WIND IS ROUND

The rose we worship has its folded rows;
They open as the wind writes pink on paper,
Then scatter, so that roses more and more
May cling to the trellises of everywhere,

Passionately twined. Thorn and petal show
The wind weighed roses as it swung the snow.
Now the wind howls; but should it sigh,
The rose would open for the open eye.

A BALCONY WITH BIRDS

The mind drowned in the sun may dream of birds,
  All downed, too heavy to arise, but when
The trees release their shuttlecocks of wings,
  Which bank of birds is but imaginings?
The eye must follow form, but from this height,
  I see how softly summer parries weight
Till everything alive weighs less and less
  And, thinly felt, the weighted consciousness,

No thicker than green leaves, or the meridian,
  Grows thinner, even, to absorb the sun.
All heaviness goes up, and up the clouds—
  Those thin patricians thick as Roman crowds
Assumpted in white togas into blue—
  Yet, painful in the light, the real, in view,
Drifts back to the roof and the ailanthus tree—
  Fern of impermanence, but heavenly.

[150]

The light that hangs in the ailanthus weaves
 The leaves' leavetaking overtaking leaves.
The actual is real and not imagined—still,
 The eye, so learned in disenchantment, sees
Two trees at once, this one of summer's will,
 And winter's one, when no bird will assail
The skyline's hyaline transparencies,
 Emptying its architecture by degrees.

Roundly in its fury, soon, the sun,
 Feverish with light, goes down, and on
Come ambitious stars—the stars that were
 But this morning dimmed. Somewhere a slow
Piano scales the summits of the air
 And disappears, and dark descends, and though
The birds turn off their songs now light is gone,
 The mind drowned in the dark may dream them on.

THE SEA GOD

Divinities unroll
From sea foil, none divine
   For me, but one I call,
True gods, my very own,
   Whose body I still see
Rolled blue in summer sun,
   Whose waters made of me
His only one.

At the breakers' plunge,
Steep in his corridors,
   No other gods expunge
My image from his mirrors,
   For I have come to be
His shadowy cardinal,
   Priesting on his sea,
And his, all.

TORCHES

(*For Gene Baro*)

Whatever light may hold,
Time catches and lets go. The net
    Trembles in fire, and yet
A darkening slackness is foretold.

    Turn every lamp up high!
Yet something secret still will stir,
    Eluding the listener,
And inaccessible to the eye.

    Who is that riddling ghost
Who haunts not houses but all men,
    And comes, again and again,
Neither desire's guest nor the host

Of will? It is dark thought,
Whose winged illumination
   Nests in the brain alone,
A phoenix rising, but unsought.

   Knowing we cannot know
What current moves us, or when light
   Will fade into its night,
Saying, it is time to go,

   We kindle the black air;
Mute figures struggle far below,
   Murdering logic, though
The sun is up, and torches flare.

VII

A SUMMER GONE

(For Mildred Wood)

I

The brilliant seaside glitters its farewell
To bathers who pack up their stripes and go
Home from all the cottages that water built;
Deserted on deserted dunes, those stilts
Of slipshod timber watch the sun run out
Among their crooked legs to meet the sea.
The windows, darker as the days go by,
Drink in the liquor of the autumn light.

II

The spiral shells, now empty of their hosts
That noiselessly would hunt the sands at night,
Are not more empty than a house I know
Whose windows, boarded up, are black with dark.
The inner and the outer night converge

On blind astronomers who used to search
The summer sky for stars. The stars that fall,
In quick succession, are not seen at all.

III

Say there was a tree that once you loved
That storms drilled downward. It was but a sign
Of how the seasons wither in a man.
Its leaves will spring into your winter mind,
Until your mind's a winter lacking spring,
Until your mind is nothing but a spring
That feeds the network of another tree
That storms will work at till the roots are free.

IV

Intrinsic as the crickets are to night,
The summer night is music made by them.
Uncritical, we listen to their themes.
The little orchestras that lure the stars
Down, down from fiery perimeters
Until we seem to touch them with our hands,
Have chirped into a silence. Where are they
Who plucked the hours of our sleep away?

V

Is it love that makes our summers shine?
Ideas of love, I mean. The naked limbs:
Bronze gears that cut the bluest sky to shreds
By running past reclining, sandy heads?
Sweet breasts that hold the very heart of love?
All shapely weights that we are mad to love?
Those beautiful outsides, those thin-skinned maps
Are part of love. Or all of it, perhaps.

VI

The insects scatter on their flimsy wings
And disappear. Sometimes one finds a trace
Of one, and sees a wingless carapace
Erosion has a mind to sculpture in.
Such tiny fans, fantastic skins are they,
One cannot hold them in the hand. The wind
Will bear, invisible upon the air,
Those cenotaphs to nothingness away.

VII

If you have listened to a summer rain,
You cannot think it will not come again:
Dead thunder that put tonnage in a drum,
Light rummaging to crack its fork on sky;
If, sleeping on a sun porch rinsed by rain.
(A vine of morning-glories climbed the pane
Outside), you plumbed the very depths of sleep,
You know the silences through which sound seeps.

VIII

Sea purses lie on the September beach,
Miniature, old-fashioned sleds of black,
The runners clawlike, paired parentheses.
These are egg cases of the skate or shark,
And if they ever held their dangerous young,
Indented by the hand, like dry seaweed,
The horny little shapes hold nothing now.
Each is an artifact that you can hold.

IX

There is a time when feeling knows two things:
The dead bird lying, and the whir of wings.
Those travelers who beat the upper air
Have clarities in mind—a south somewhere,
Where clouds are higher and the sea more blue.
Diviners of the tropics have to go
Where summer is still spoken. Autumn wings
Time the distances between two things.

X

Sad fall, a thousand dyings color you:
The sunburnt skin of leaves. Of love, the view
To take is but another wintry one,
To wait for the new nestings of the sun.
Happy for the leaves that make us sad,
We walk across your fields of richest plaid,
Grateful for the view. We'll have, someday,
That other weather that we salt away.

NOTE

From *The Wound and the Weather, 1946:* THE SWAN,
CLICHÉS FOR PIANO AND ORCHESTRA, AS SUNLIGHT'S FEVER,
WATERWALL BLUES, A PORTRAIT, AROUND THE FISH.

From *The Toy Fair, 1954:* A STREET WITH CHILDREN, ELEGY
FOR MY FATHER, ADOLESCENT'S SONG, A LESSON FROM VAN
GOGH, ADVICE TO A TRAVELER, CRY FROM MONTAUK, THE
HERMIT, THE SKIERS, BERMUDA, MARINER'S SONG, MOUN-
TAIN AND CLOUDS, VENICE, BURNING LOVE LETTERS, SONG,
THE VIEW MINUS ONE, THE LIE, ROMANTIC LOVE: A FOOT-
NOTE, WINTER'S END, ELIZABETHAN TRAGEDY: A FOOTNOTE,
SALT-WATER TAFFY, THE WIND IS ROUND, A BALCONY
WITH BIRDS.

From *A Swimmer in the Air, 1957:* A WINTER COME, THOSE
WHO CANNOT ARE CONDEMNED, HORROR MOVIE, TRAGEDY,
A SWIMMER IN THE AIR, THE GIFT TO BE SIMPLE, A BOX
AT THE OPERA, LETTER TO AN IMAGINARY BRAZIL, LOCAL
PLACES, THE FALLS OF LOVE, RAIN, SMALL ELEGY, A MAR-
RIAGE, CHALK FROM EDEN, ROUNDS, UNDERWOOD, SKIN AND
BONE, A SUMMER GONE.

New Poems: DREAMS, THE DUMB SHOW, FLORIDA, TOURISTS,
EXPLORERS, KING MIDAS, IF YOU CAN, THE TRUTH ABOUT
LOVE, A SONG STRUCK FROM THE RECORDS, THE FEAST, LIGHT
AND DARK, PINE, THE SEA GOD, TORCHES.